T5-AQT-719

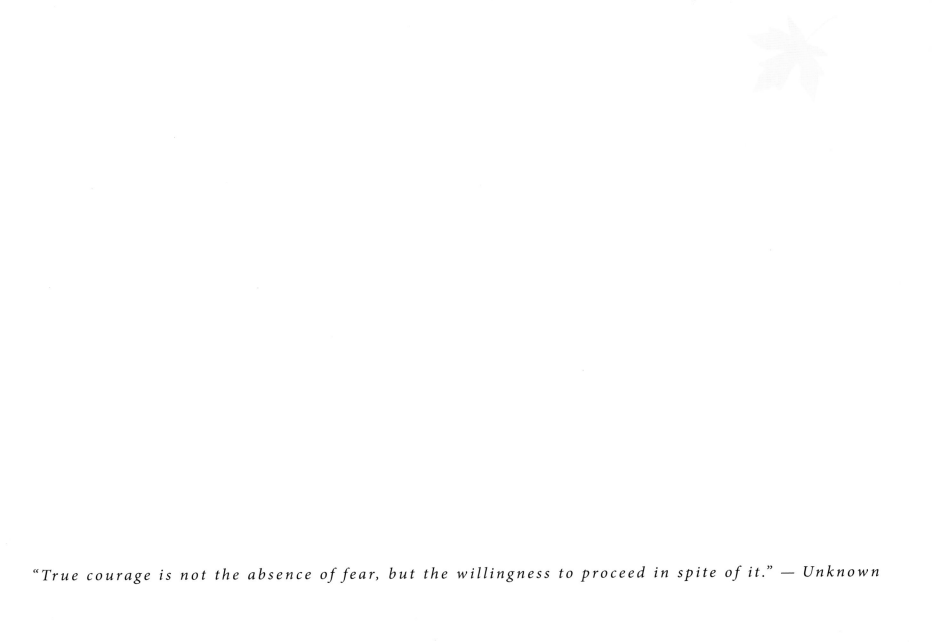

"*True courage is not the absence of fear, but the willingness to proceed in spite of it.*" — *Unknown*

Healing Images

A Selection from the Lemmen-Holton Cancer Pavilion

PHOTOGRAPHY BY STACY A. NIEDZWIECKI

FOREWORD BY RICHARD J. FUNNELL, MHA, FACHE, CMPE

Previous spread:

Reflections of Autumn

PICKEREL LAKE, KENT COUNTY, MICHIGAN

Copyright © 2010 by Spectrum Health. All rights reserved.

This 2010 edition published by Spectrum Health Innovations.

All rights reserved under international and Pan-American copyright conventions.
No part of this publication may be reproduced, stored in a retrieval system, or transmitted
in any form or by any means, electronic, mechanical, photocopying, recording or otherwise,
without prior written permission from the publisher.

Spectrum Health Innovations
100 Michigan St. NE
Grand Rapids, MI 49503

ISBN: 978-0-9843746-0-1

Printed and bound in the United States of America by Color House Graphics, Grand Rapids, Michigan.

Acknowledgements

Photography and introduction: Copyright © 2006, 2007, 2008 and 2009 by Stacy A. Niedzwiecki

Foreword: Copyright © 2009 by Richard J. Funnell, MHA, FACHE, CMPE

Book design: Stacy A. Niedzwiecki

Interior pages: Printed on Forest Stewardship Council (FSC) certified text stock

To order prints of images: StacyN.com

First published: February 2010

Art plays a key role in the healing journey. It provides a connection to the patient that speaks its own language. It allows patients to personalize the art to their own healing experience. Healing art is a spiritual path, a transformational process, a way of being. It unites the mind, body and spirit. The artwork at Spectrum Health Lemmen-Holton Cancer Pavilion is purposeful, offering nourishment for the soul and providing each patient with hope and encouragement during the healing process. It is our desire that this book will continue to be a reminder of the patient's connection to life through the healing experience.

Richard J. Funnell MHA, FACHE, CMPE
SENIOR DIRECTOR, ONCOLOGY PROGRAM

ABOUT THE LEMMEN-HOLTON CANCER PAVILION

This state-of-the-art facility delivers West Michigan's widest, most advanced array of outpatient cancer services—treating more than 70 percent of all new adult cancer cases in Kent County alone. Designed with input from former patients and cancer experts, the pavilion offers a warm, soothing environment for exceptional and compassionate patient care.

A Perfect Garden
NEAR MANCHESTER, VERMONT

Welcome, friend . . . I hope these images give you *much* to celebrate about life!

Upon learning my photographs would hang in the new Lemmen-Holton Cancer Pavilion, I wavered between sheer joy and absolute panic. It was the honor of a lifetime, but I also questioned if I was up to the challenge. There were numerous moments of self-doubt. I often wondered, "What if …?"

People who experience cancer face the same "what if" challenge every day. It motivated me to confront my barriers to help reinforce the astonishing strength of people affected by cancer—not just patients, but also families, caregivers and hospital staff.

Art, particularly scenes of nature's splendor, can provide a calming, nurturing environment at times when it is needed most. It didn't take long to work past my fears to realize others' more urgent needs. I'm delighted to present my work alongside that of many other talented artists in a therapeutic setting created to stimulate healing of the body, mind and spirit.

The original intent of this book was to help in the healing journey of cancer patients. However, clinical research has shown art is extremely beneficial in healing a variety of conditions, including stress. Photographing these scenes made me deeply happy—my goal is to share that joy with you.

9

Stacy A. Niedzwiecki

PHOTOGRAPHER

Suspended Bliss

OLD MISSION PENINSULA, MICHIGAN

The Mighty Mac

MACKINAW CITY, MICHIGAN

Old Mackinac Point Lighthouse

MACKINAW CITY, MICHIGAN

Little Sable Lighthouse

White River Light Station

WHITEHALL, MICHIGAN

A Summer Day

MEINERT COUNTY PARK, MICHIGAN

Gala of Grass

SLEEPING BEAR DUNES NATIONAL LAKESHORE, MICHIGAN

Torch Lake

ALDEN, MICHIGAN

22

24

Old Mission Lighthouse

OLD MISSION PENINSULA, MICHIGAN

25

Morning at the Beach

EMPIRE, MICHIGAN

Marina Stroll

TRAVERSE CITY, MICHIGAN ·

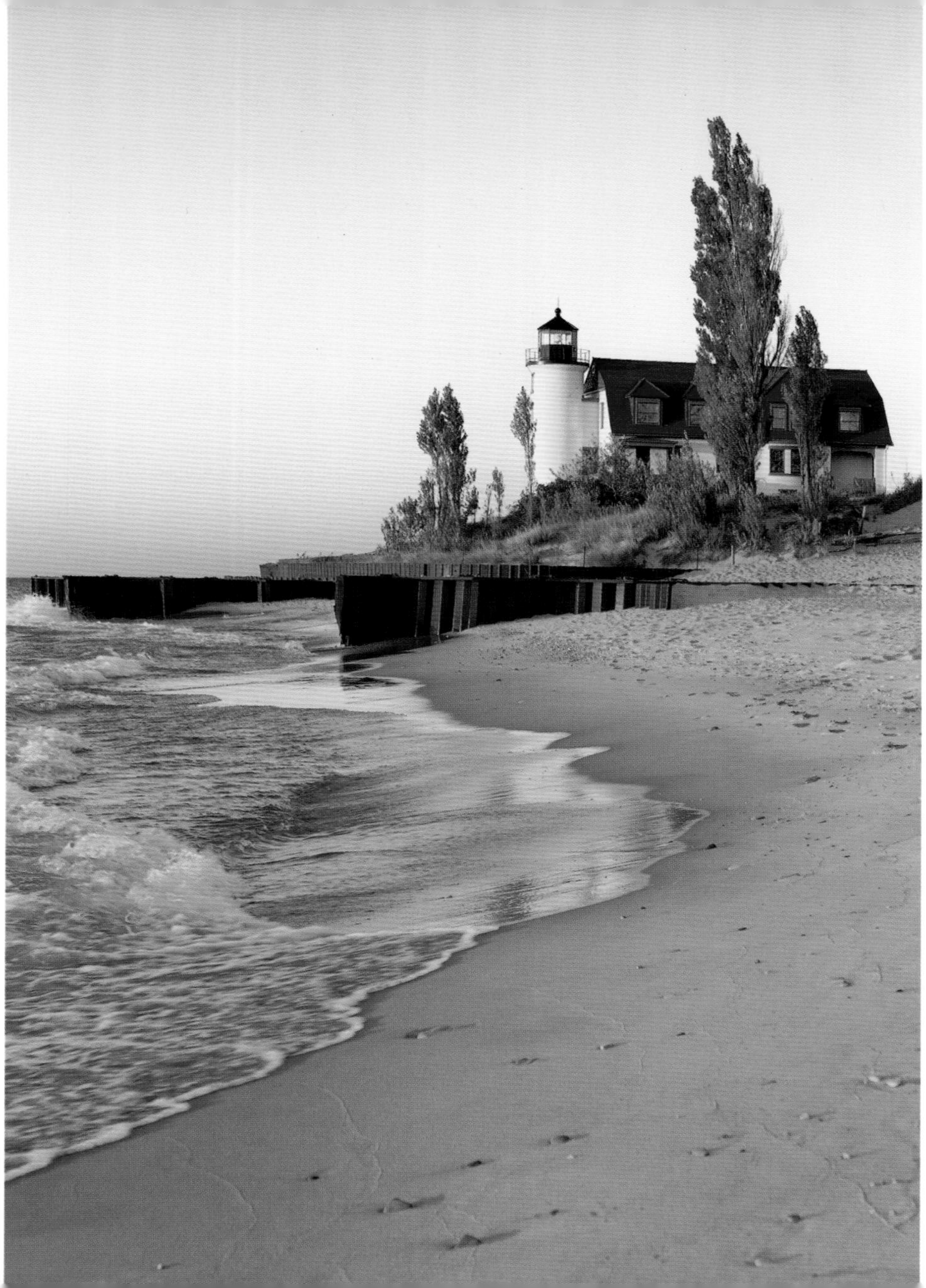

Point Betsie Lighthouse

Dechow Barn

PORT ONEIDA, MICHIGAN

View from the Bluffs

EMPIRE, MICHIGAN

Manitou View

SLEEPING BEAR DUNES NATIONAL LAKESHORE, MICHIGAN

Beaming

NEAR ADA, MICHIGAN

40

Tweddle Barn

NEAR EMPIRE, MICHIGAN

41

42

Basch Farm

PORT ONEIDA, MICHIGAN

44

Lakeside Afternoon

REEDS LAKE, EAST GRAND RAPIDS, MICHIGAN

Holiday Regatta

REEDS LAKE, EAST GRAND RAPIDS, MICHIGAN

47

Mr. Oriole

COURTLAND TOWNSHIP, MICHIGAN

49

Perfection

LITTLE BOSTWICK LAKE, MICHIGAN

After the Rain

54

Empire Beach

EMPIRE, MICHIGAN

55

The Tree of Light

CANNONSBURG, MICHIGAN

Snowfall

FALLASBURG COVERED BRIDGE NEAR LOWELL, MICHIGAN

Holy Cow

ST. PATRICK'S, PARNELL, MICHIGAN

Wild Waves

GRAND HAVEN, MICHIGAN

The Chosen Path

CANNON TOWNSHIP, MICHIGAN

Fallasburg Barn

Grand Rapids at Dusk

AH-NAB-AWEN PARK, GRAND RAPIDS, MICHIGAN

Celebration on the Grand

GRAND RAPIDS, MICHIGAN

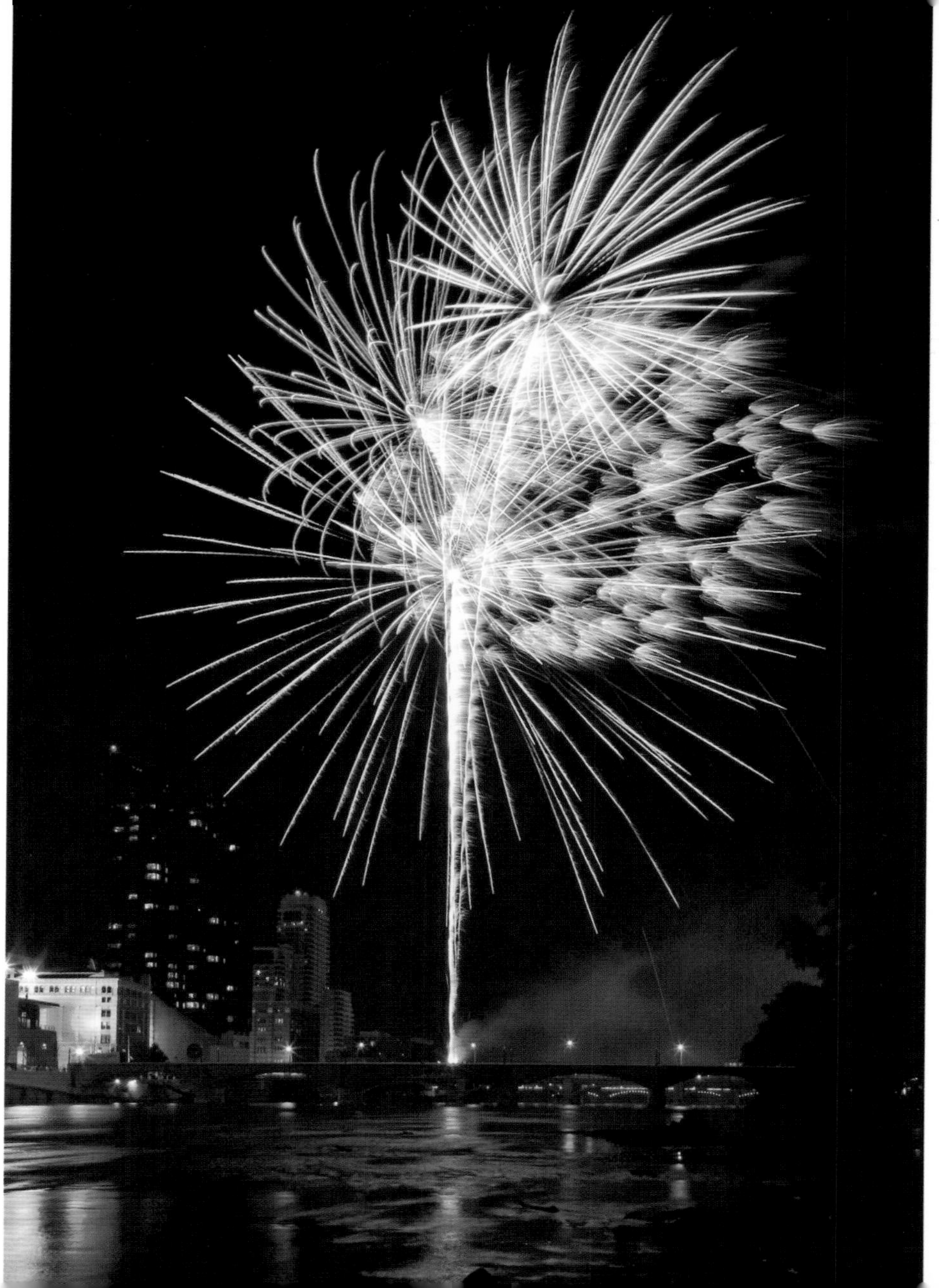

North Manitou Island

VIEW FROM GLEN HAVEN, MICHIGAN

Tiger Swallowtail

COURTLAND TOWNSHIP, MICHIGAN

American Copper

ROCKFORD, MICHIGAN

Karner Blue

ROCKFORD, MICHIGAN

Mute Swan

CANNONSBURG, MICHIGAN

Two for Tulips

HOLLAND, MICHIGAN

Daybreak Clouds

SLEEPING BEAR DUNES NATIONAL LAKESHORE, MICHIGAN

Spring at Fallasburg Bridge

VERGENNES TOWNSHIP, MICHIGAN

83

Prepare for Liftoff

COURTLAND TOWNSHIP, MICHIGAN

Take Your Seat

SLEEPING BEAR DUNES NATIONAL LAKESHORE, MICHIGAN

Pedals

INDIAN RIVER, MICHIGAN

Thoreson Farm

PORT ONEIDA, MICHIGAN

Naturally Yours

SPENCER TOWNSHIP, MICHIGAN

94

Afternoon Snack

COURTLAND TOWNSHIP, MICHIGAN

A Great Lake

LAKE MICHIGAN AT SLEEPING BEAR DUNES

97

Big Red

HOLLAND STATE PARK, MICHIGAN

100

Lovely Lupine

101

D.H. Day Farm

SLEEPING BEAR DUNES NATIONAL LAKESHORE, MICHIGAN

104

Sleeping Bear Bay
PORT ONEIDA, MICHIGAN

Spring at Honey Creek

ADA, MICHIGAN

Serenity

PETERSON PARK, LEELANAU PENINSULA, MICHIGAN

Index